Anxiety

Reduce your stress, concentrate, and revitalize your spirit.

SEAMALL BREE

Table of Contents

A general introduction to anxiety:

An overview

What causes you to feel anxious when you have to take a test or give a presentation?

Are you experiencing feelings of anxiety when you think of attending a family reunion?

Have you noticed that you are feeling more pressured as a result of the impending deadline or the scheduled dentist appointment?

The majority of people are in agreement with you if you answered "yes" to any of the questions that came before this one. Despite the fact that people's responses to specific occurrences may vary, the reality remains that almost everyone experiences some level of worry, unease, fear, or anxiety on a daily basis.

It is a "natural feeling" to experience anxiety; the question is, when does it become something else entirely?

A diagnosis of an anxiety disorder is warranted when a person's anxious sensations (fear, concern, nervousness, etc.) do not go away or even get worse over time and interfere with their day-to-day functioning (in relation to work, school, friends, family, etc.). This is necessary in order to determine whether or not the individual is suffering from an anxiety disorder. A person who suffers from this condition may have feelings of isolation as a result of the fact that some people may not accept or even acknowledge them. Because of this, it is of the utmost importance to recognize the symptoms at an early stage, differentiate them from typical anxiety, and seek therapy as soon as possible. It is only appropriate for a skilled mental health professional, such as a psychiatrist or psychologist, to diagnose and treat difficulties related to mental health. As a result of the fact that they typically employ skilled mental health doctors who are able to provide hidden diagnosis and therapy, Indian rehabilitation facilities are excellent places to start the process of healing.

The following are the three broad categories that can be used to classify anxiety disorders:

- OCD symptoms might include issues with sleep, rituals, and other types
- Problems that are associated with stress and anxiety

- Stress-related conditions that manifest themselves in this way

In what ways could anxiety be caused by a number of different factors?

There is a significant prevalence of anxiety disorders; nevertheless, certain individuals may have a higher likelihood of developing these diseases if they are given exposure to particular risk factors. The following are some examples of potential dangers that could occur:

Genetically derived (inherited)

The significance of parents in the educational experiences of their children

Problems and catastrophes in day-to-day life, as well as a lower standard of living in terms of both economic and social status

Being a member of a community that has been oppressed throughout history

Be afflicted with a persistent chronic health condition

Abuse of substances or physical manifestations of withdrawal

Behavioral factors (including smoking and consuming an excessive amount of coffee, for example)

The relationship between anxiety and physical health

Anxiety disorders are associated with an increased risk of developing a variety of health issues, including but not limited to obesity, hypertension, and diabetes. The presence of these potentially fatal disorders can be identified by a number of indicators, including obesity, elevated levels of "bad" cholesterol, triglycerides, and blood glucose. It has been established via research that unrestrained anxiety can produce changes in fundamental biology, which can result in catastrophic medical problems. However, the precise mechanism by which anxiety causes these threats to arise is not yet known. As a result, the hypothesis that anxiety affects the complete person is given more weight by this evidence.

In the event that you observe any of these warning signs or are concerned that your anxiety is having an effect on your physical health, you have the option of consulting a physician or enrolling in one of the many detox clinics that are located in India.

To what extent is it possible to treat anxiety?

Answer in a nutshell: yes. Among the most common types of treatment, counseling and other tried-and-true therapeutic procedures are among the most popular therapies.

When attempting to conquer extreme anxiety, it may be good to consult with a counselor about probable triggers and ways for coping with the condition. The client may seek the advice of a counselor for a range of issues, including but not limited to concerns over stress, inability to effectively manage time, and difficulties in interpersonal relationships.

The profession of psychotherapy:

Throughout the course of time, a variety of additional treatments have also demonstrated promising results. Cognitive behavioral therapy (CBT), therapeutic family work, and extended exposure treatment (PE) are a few examples of the types of approaches that fall under this category. Patients who are experiencing anxiety disorders and other mental health challenges can receive therapy at the Sunshine Wellness Centre, which is one of the many drug treatment institutes in India that provide therapeutic services.

Pharmaceuticals

There is a possibility that the practitioner will decide to prescribe medication after assessing the patient's symptoms and general state of health. Medications that have been prescribed for problems such as mental health, cardiovascular health, and other conditions.

- A variety of therapeutic approaches

A typical method for relieving anxiety is to combine conventional treatment with non-invasive alternative therapies such as yoga, meditation, acupuncture, and other similar practices. Complementary treatments are offered at Sunshine Wellness Center, which is considered to be one of the top drug rehab clinics. These therapies are designed to assist patients in coping with conventional medical care rather than to replace it.

Nothing in life is ever exactly as it appears to be. The expectation that we will provide one hundred percent each and every day is not reasonable. Whatever the case may be, it is normal to experience some level of anxiousness. This is what distinguishes you from other creatures and what gives you the ability to be considered human.

An explanation of the cognitive-behavioral therapy (CBT) definition

If you could help describe what cognitive behavioral therapy is and how it is employed, I would really appreciate it. Cognitive-behavioral therapy (CBT) is a form of psychotherapy that aims to enhance patients' emotional and behavioral well-being by teaching them to become more self-aware and to change the negative thought patterns that they have developed over time.

- The Concise Definition of CBT

"Cognitive-behavioral therapy" is a form of therapy that includes elements of both behavioral and cognitive therapies with the intention of assisting patients in "identifying incorrect or maladaptive patterns of thought, emotional reaction, or behavior and replacing them with desired patterns."

When it comes to emotional instability, despair, and anxiety, cognitive behavioral therapy places a significant emphasis on recognizing and correcting negative thought patterns that either contribute to or exacerbate these characteristics. At the same time as they emerge seemingly out of nowhere, these negative notions have a detrimental effect on our demeanor.

Identification of illogical ideas, questioning of those beliefs, and ultimately the replacement of those beliefs with ones that are more reasonable and sensible are all components of cognitive behavioral therapy (CBT).

This book provides a concise overview of cognitive behavioral therapy (CBT) in only one minute and thirty-one seconds. The film has been evaluated by Steven Gans, MD, to see whether or not it is accurate from a medical standpoint. There are numerous variations of cognitive behavioral therapy.

In cognitive behavioral therapy (CBT), which is used to deal with our thoughts, feelings, and actions, there is a wide variety of methods and approaches that are utilized. Structured psychotherapies and self-help techniques are two examples of alternative approaches. The application of cognitive-behavioral therapy can be seen in a wide variety of therapeutic settings. The basic purpose of cognitive therapy is to identify and modify dysfunctional patterns of thinking, feeling, and behaving when they are identified and addressed.

By teaching patients skills such as emotional regulation and mindfulness, dialectical behavior therapy (DBT) aims to assist patients in breaking damaging patterns of thought and behavior. This is accomplished by teaching patients skills.

The principles of multimodal treatment are the seven distinct but interconnected domains of behavior, emotion, sensation, imagery, cognition, interpersonal variables, medication, and biology. These are the fundamentals of multimodal treatment that, when applied to mental health concerns, produce the best results. Individuals who participate in rational emotive behavior therapy (REBT) acquire the ability to identify negative thought patterns and then challenge the validity of those patterns in order to modify them.

Despite the fact that they focus on different aspects of mental distress, all forms of cognitive behavioral therapy (CBT) are centered on the modification of dysfunctional ways of thinking.

- Techniques of treatment that are both behavioral and cognitive

Beyond the simple identification of thought patterns, cognitive behavioral therapy involves a wider range of activities. He makes use of a wide variety of approaches in order to assist individuals in overcoming these tendencies. A few cognitive behavioral therapy (CBT) approaches are described in the following paragraphs.

Some suggestions that are not productive. Having an understanding of the ways in which illogical behavior can be influenced by unpleasant thoughts, feelings, and experiences is of the utmost significance.

It is possible, however, that it will be difficult, particularly for people who have difficulty engaging in reflection. Recognizing these thoughts can lead to increased self-awareness and comprehension, whilst ignoring them can delay the process of rehabilitation.

- Implementing theoretical frameworks in practice

A common component of cognitive behavioral therapy is the teaching of skills that may be applied in real-world situations and situations that occur in everyday life. It is possible, for instance, that a person's coping techniques for social situations that cause relapses are similar to those of a person who suffers from a substance use disorder.

- Putting together a list of

During the process of recovery from mental illness, one of the most effective methods to maintain motivation is to establish goals that are both clear and accessible. In cognitive behavioral therapy, one of the most significant aspects is the therapist's ability to assist in the development and reinforcement of the client's ability to define goals.

One technique that might be taken is to educate you the nuances of goal identification, as well as to assist you in distinguishing between short-term and long-term targets. When it comes to goals, SMART goals—that is, goals that are specified, measurable, achievable, relevant, and time-bound—will give the process the same amount of weight as they do the final result.

- Finding solutions to issues

The techniques that are taught in cognitive behavioral therapy can be utilized to find solutions to a wide variety of issues that arise in one's life. When this is done, diseases, both mental and physical, have the potential to have less of an impact on the lives of individuals involved.

The following five steps need to be taken in order to fix frequent problems with cognitive behavioral therapy (CBT):

Locate the source of the issue. Try to come up with a few different solutions to the problem. Carefully consider each alternative, both the positive and negative aspects of each one. Choose a strategy to put into action. Take the necessary steps to remedy the problem.

- The tracking of individuals

The practice of self-monitoring, which can be accomplished through the use of a notebook, is an essential component of cognitive behavioral therapy. Your therapist should be informed of your findings and progress while you are keeping a diary of your activities, symptoms, or experiences over the course of multiple sessions. Your therapist will be able to provide you with better assistance if you provide them with data from your own self-monitoring. For those who battle with eating disorders, it may be beneficial to keep a food journal that details their typical eating times as well as the feelings they experience in the minutes leading up to, during, and after meals.

Activities such as keeping a journal, participating in role-playing, practicing relaxation techniques, and adding mental diversions are all ways in which you can improve the effectiveness of your cognitive behavioral therapy (CBT) program. Typical outcomes that can be anticipated from cognitive behavioral therapy Cognitive behavioral therapy is a form of treatment that requires only a short period of time and can assist individuals in learning to pay attention to their thoughts and beliefs in the here and now. There is a vast variety of medical disorders that can be treated using cognitive behavioral therapy's use.

It is important to note that the advantages of cognitive-behavioral treatment are not limited to the field of mental health.

- The presence of persistent pain or a crucial health concern
- Splitting up and getting divorced
- Despair following the occurrence of a setback

- The Nightmare That Is Lack confidence in oneself
  Relationships that are in conflict
- During times of stress, some suggestions for self-care

TCC CBT is based on the assumption that an individual's mental state has a significant impact on their behavior, which is one of the benefits of the treatment.

As a result of their persistent anxiety regarding potential disasters, such as airplane crashes and runway accidents, some individuals may decide to abstain from flying altogether.

Cognitive-behavioral therapy can assist individuals in becoming more self-aware and in accepting responsibility for their responses and interpretations of their experiences, despite the fact that they may not be able to influence the external circumstances in which they find themselves.

The following is a list of the more significant benefits that cognitive behavioral therapy offers: Through the process of exposing and addressing unpleasant, emotionally draining thoughts, this strategy can assist you in replacing those thoughts with positive, productive ones rather than the negative ones.

As a form of therapy that is relatively short-term, it often only takes anywhere from five to twenty sessions to observe results.

It can be beneficial to a wide variety of undesirable habits. The cost is typically lower than the cost of alternative treatment choices in the majority of cases. The treatment is successful regardless of whether it is administered in person or online.

This treatment option is available to individuals who do not require the use of psychiatric drugs. Cognitive behavioral therapy, also known as CBT, is a form of treatment that teaches individuals methods that they can use in the present as well as in the future in order to overcome the challenges they are facing.

Arguments in Support of Cognitive Behavioral Therapy

During the 1960s, a psychiatrist named Aaron Beck made the discovery that particular patterns of thinking made the emotional issues of his patients even more severe. This understanding ultimately led to the development of cognitive behavioral therapy (CBT). The issue of "automatic negative thoughts" was the impetus for Beck to develop cognitive therapy as a potential treatment option.

In contrast to the practically exclusive use of associations, reinforcing, and punishments in traditional behavioral therapies, the cognitive approach seeks to improve behavior by concentrating on the ways in which an individual's thoughts and feelings influence that behavior.

The cognitive-behavioral approach is currently one of the treatments that has received the greatest attention from researchers. The application of this method has demonstrated positive outcomes in the treatment of a wide variety of mental health conditions, such as anxiety, depression, eating disorders, insomnia, obsessive-compulsive disorder, post-traumatic stress disorder, and substance abuse. Cognitive behavioral therapy has been shown to be the most effective method for treating eating problems, according to medical study. Cognitive-behavioral therapy (CBT) may be able to provide assistance to individuals who have trouble sleeping as a result of medical issues such as chronic pain or mood disorders such as depression.

In the treatment of anxiety and depression in children and adolescents, cognitive behavioral therapy has been shown to be effective. Anxiety and anxiety-related diseases, such as post-traumatic stress disorder (PTSD) and obsessive-compulsive disorder, were found to demonstrate clinically significant benefits, according to a meta-analysis conducted in 2018 that included 41 trials.

When it comes to assisting those who are struggling with issues related to substance usage, cognitive behavioral therapy has received a great deal of support from research. The available evidence suggests that this type of treatment can assist individuals who are battling substance use disorders in the development of improved coping skills, the acquisition of the ability to manage their urges, and the reduction of their exposure to situations that trigger their symptoms. Cognitive Behavioral Therapy (CBT) is one of the therapies that has received the most research since it is centered on the accomplishment of particular objectives and has outcomes that can be measured.

According to the results of a survey titled "Mind's Cost of Treatment," which intended to gain a better understanding of how people in the United States deal with the financial obstacles that are involved with therapy, a significant majority of respondents felt that treatment is beneficial. Roughly ninety percent of respondents believe that the recommendation is beneficial.

84% of patients are satisfied with how far they have progressed in treatment, and 91% are satisfied with the therapy itself. This is in reference to the patients' mental health.

- Considerations That Are Crucial When It Comes to Cognitive Behavioral Therapy

It is possible that some individuals will find it challenging to execute cognitive behavioral therapy. Listed below are some examples for your perusal. Adapt to the ever-changing circumstances. Although they are aware of their negative thinking patterns, some patients report feeling trapped when they first begin treatment. This is because they are unable to change their negative thought patterns. The structure of cognitive behavioral therapy is really nice. One of the key differences between cognitive behavioral therapy and psychoanalytic psychotherapy is that the former does not place a high priority on addressing the patient's underlying resistance to change. A 15 On the other hand, it is more structured, which may provide difficulties for people who are trying to maintain order in their activities.

Having the ability to adjust is crucial. To ensure that cognitive behavioral therapy is successful, you must be willing to devote a considerable amount of time to introspection into your own actions and behaviors. To comprehend the manner in which our feelings impact our actions, it is necessary to engage in introspection, which is not always an easy task. The completion of tasks often requires a certain amount of time. The cognitive behavioral therapy (CBT) approach is often one that helps with modifying behavior in a progressive and step-by-step manner over the course of a significant amount of time. When a patient is in the beginning phases of treatment for social anxiety, for example, it may be beneficial for them to mentally recreate unpleasant social situations when they are doing so. Joining forces with dependable friends or family members can be the next move that makes the most sense. When you work on tiny goals that contribute to a larger one, it is much simpler to deal with the situations that arise.

Beginning Cognitive Behavioral Therapy: Where to Start

The cognitive behavioral therapy approach has proven to be effective in treating a variety of mental health issues. The following should be taken into consideration in order to determine whether or not this treatment could be beneficial for you or a loved one:

It is easy to find a qualified therapist by either seeking a reference from your primary care physician or by looking through the registry of accredited practitioners maintained by the National Association of Cognitive-Behavioral Therapists. Your search for "cognitive behavioral therapy near me" will also yield results for practitioners of this method who are located in your immediate vicinity.

You should give some thought to your individual preferences, such as whether you believe that having treatment in person or electronically would be more beneficial to you.

It is essential to get in touch with your insurance provider in order to obtain information regarding the number of sessions of cognitive behavioral therapy that are reimbursed annually.

You should put a note in your calendar and schedule an appointment with the therapist of your choice. Be eager and bring a pleasant attitude to the initial meeting you have with the other person. It is time to stop squandering time and begin making progress; in order to accomplish this, you need to be ready to recognize the elements that have been keeping you from accomplishing your objectives.

- As You Consider Cognitive Behavioral Therapy

Here Are Some Things You Should Expect As someone who has never participated in cognitive behavioral therapy (CBT), you might be curious about how the treatment operates. It is expected that this session would be structured in the same manner as your initial consultation with any other physician.

At the beginning of the session, the therapist and the patient will normally go over a therapist-patient service agreement, information regarding insurance, the patient's medical history, the drugs that are currently being taken, and HIPAA documentation also known as privacy documents. Over the course of the virtual consultation, it is quite likely that these forms will be filled out electronically.

In order to get to the bottom of your symptoms and determine what caused them, your physician will most likely ask you a lot of personal questions about your current health. These inquiries will include information about your upbringing, education, employment, connections (romantic, familial, and friends), and other aspects of your life. prompted you to look for assistance. Your cognitive behavioral therapist will be more positioned to aid you in being more self-aware of your own harmful or unrealistic thought patterns once they have gained a deeper understanding of you, your challenges, and what you wish to achieve through cognitive behavioral therapy (CBT). You have to begin thinking and behaving in a more optimistic manner; hence, the following stage is to begin employing strategies that will effectively accomplish this goal.

We will discuss the approaches that have been successful as well as those that have not been successful in the upcoming meetings. One example of a self-help cognitive behavioral therapy (CBT) activity that your therapist might recommend is keeping a journal in which you record negative thoughts or performing exercises designed to reduce anxiety in between sessions.

What's wrong with me?

Ever wondered, "What's wrong with me?" at any point in your life? Have you ever asked yourself that question? You are not the only one, then. There is a good chance that you have already found yourself thinking about this. While insecurities may only last for a short period of time for some people, they may do so for the entirety of their lives for others. Furthermore, it may be an indication that you are currently confronted with a situation that leads you to question your capacity to endure.

Regardless of the origin of your uncertainties, you should be aware that there are actions you can do to start feeling differently about yourself. In addition, you shouldn't try to ignore this feeling when it comes to you; you should just accept it. Sit with your feelings rather than trying to put them to the side when you are experiencing them. It is possible that it might be beneficial to discuss your mental suffering with a trained expert, even if the idea of doing so is frightening.

The causes of your unease, as well as nine simple methods to restore your equilibrium You need to determine the source of your skepticism before you can even begin to discuss potential therapies. This discomfort could be the result of a variety of factors, ranging from a momentary setback to a more fundamental medical ailment. Check out the scenarios and see if any of them sound like something you've experienced before.

Having a feeling of being overpowered One of the most frequent responses to the possibility that anything might be wrong with you is to experience feelings of being overwhelmed or to be unable to think clearly. Additionally, do you ever get the impression that there are simply too many things you need to get done, but you don't have enough time to get them done? If you are experiencing feelings of illness, it may be because of the exceedingly difficult circumstances in which you are living. There are several activities and circumstances that can give you the impression that you are slipping behind in the speed of life. Having a stressful career, a large family, financial difficulties, or anything else along those lines are examples of these types of circumstances.

Have you ever had the experience of feeling as though you are at a halt, even when everything around you seems to be going swimmingly? You might, on the other hand, be trying to move on from a relationship that is traumatic to you, a job that you despise, or a breakup relationship. When you are unsatisfied with your current circumstance because you compare it to your idealized image of it, it is obvious that there is something wrong with you.

The ability to break through a deadlock situation
Disengaged and feeling depressed

The feelings of isolation and loneliness can be brought on by a variety of factors. On the other side, it's possible that you have difficulty expressing yourself to the people you care about or that you can be bashful around new people. When one dwells on the negative ideas that come with being alone, it becomes more difficult to cultivate the kind of profound friendships and romantic relationships that are beneficial to one's health and lifespan.

Start right away by carrying out these ten easy steps! Isolation brought on by One's Experiences of Trauma

It is possible that you are dealing with the aftermath of a traumatic experience if you are having concerns about your health. A person might experience trauma in a variety of ways, such as the loss of a loved one, being physically abused, or experiencing a catastrophic incident such as a house fire.

As real, if not more so, is the experience of living with a narcissistic abuser or any other cause of trauma that is subtle and covert. If you or someone you know has been through any kind of traumatic situation, it is strongly suggested that you seek the support of a mental health expert. Having a physical sickness and being sick with it When you look at yourself, do you get the feeling that something is amiss with your physical appearance? You are undoubtedly feeling confused and anxious about what is going on, regardless of whether you have a medical problem that has been recorded in the past and are now having new symptoms or whether your symptoms have not been recognized or diagnosed. affects the state of your physical health.

If you are wondering, "What's wrong with me?" considering the circumstances, we completely understand your question. A accurate diagnosis from a medical professional is frequently the initial step in the process of resolving a problem. Have a negative impact on one's sense of the self-worth.

For those who struggle with low self-esteem, it is possible that they will begin to believe that they are faulty. It is not the validity of this feeling in relation to reality that is important; what is important is how you perceive yourself. When you treat yourself with contempt and indifference, it is impossible not to have feelings of inadequacy in every aspect of your life. In order to overcome low self-esteem, a common and effective technique is to evaluate one's underlying principles to determine whether or not they are the cause of the problem. In order to deal with mental illness and low self-esteem, there are five steps that need be taken. The constant feeling that something is wrong with you may, in the end, be the outcome of a diagnosable mental illness such as depression, anxiety, or a personality disorder.

One possible explanation for this feeling is possible.

The best course of action in these kinds of situations is to consult with a mental health professional for examination and treatment, in a manner analogous to that of a physical condition. On the other hand, you should also concentrate on developing your ability to cope with stressful situations in order to be able to take responsibility for your mental health to the fullest extent possible.

A Guide on Dealing with Difficult Circumstances and Confrontations

You have a number of options available to you in order to ease the feeling that something is wrong with you, regardless of what it is that is causing you to have that emotion. It is important to determine the source of the issue so that you may select the most appropriate strategy for fixing it. Take some time to relax and decompress. There is a possibility that the sudden realization that something is wrong could start off a chain reaction of negative feelings and ideas. Begin by engaging in activities that will make you feel good about yourself.

When it is necessary for this to take place, you should create a paper titled **"quiet activities"** and use it as a reference. Among the items that could be included on such a list to reduce stress are the ones that are listed below.

You should get out your list and start going through the items on it one by one if you find yourself feeling overwhelmed or disappointed.

- Norms that are calming

Enjoy the fresh air and sunshine by going outside. Maintain a journal in which you can write your feelings throughout the day.

It is recommended that a compassionate friend, acquaintance, or loved one be called. Consider making a list of all the things that need to be done if you are experiencing feelings of being overwhelmed and are unclear how to get started.

If you have trouble relaxing, you might find it helpful to use an app like Headspace. The therapeutic effect of inhaling the aroma of an essential oil, such as lavender, can be achieved by doing so.

Consider signing up for a yoga or relaxation class that is offered online. Investing yourself in a riveting book is a great way to get away from your feelings.

Put on a movie or television show that you enjoy watching, such as one that is calming, interesting, or both.

Make a strategy for it.

The next step is to determine how you are going to cope with the things that are truly causing you to feel horrible about yourself. In spite of the fact that it is simple to give in to hopelessness when things are difficult, maintaining your concentration on finding answers will provide you with the strength to keep going as you go. Any further action that you choose to take will be contingent on the specifics of your situation; nonetheless, it could involve any of the following opportunities:

Seek the advice of a mental health professional by consulting with them.

Find a career that allows you to make the most of your skills and experience.

You should make an effort to improve your ability in social interactions, including those with friends, romantic partners, and family relationships. Participate in activities that satisfy your desire for pleasure, such as learning to knit or participating in a sport.

The act of reading books on self-help can teach you a great deal about life and about yourself. You should look for a companion who is accountable if you need assistance remaining on track. Make time for your own self-care.

Following the completion of a few deep breaths and the formulation of a strategy to deal with the challenges you are currently facing, you are now obligated to keep a close eye on your emotions moving forward in order to put an end to a downward spiral in your mood before it becomes out of control.

By being more in tune with the signals that your body sends you, you may be able to engage in activities that improve your mood. In the event that you are experiencing any of these emotions, the following are some strategies that can help you deal with them.

In the event that you are feeling mental fogginess or overload, it may be beneficial to make a list of everything that comes to mind. Feeling completely spent: You can achieve a healthy sleep-wake cycle by doing things like going to bed and getting up at the same times every day. This will help you achieve a balance between sleeping too much and sleeping too little.

Relatively easily agitated or restless? Get out of the home and engage in some form of physical activity, such as yoga, high-intensity interval training, or walking on a treadmill.

It is important to determine the source of the pain as soon as it begins and seek relief from it as soon as possible, such as by going to the doctor. Mindfulness meditation, progressive muscle relaxation (PMR), and activities that focus on deep breathing can be beneficial for individuals who struggle to relax and experience anxiety. You should set a timer for your anxiety. Keeping track of your mental health in the same manner that you monitor your physical health is something that you should do whenever possible. The practice of setting aside time on a daily basis to reflect on and record your issues is one approach that can be used in this regard.

Following that, you will need to devise a strategy to address each of the issues. You might want to reconsider your strategy if you are concerned that you are making the situation even more difficult. The best way to ensure that you have time in your day to jot down your concerns is to schedule a certain time each day. You should set a timer and utilize it on a regular basis; when the timer goes off, you should put your troubles on hold until the next time you worry about them.

Aim to avoid dwelling on the issues that you are experiencing while you are experiencing feelings of anxiety. Take notes on your concerns, explore for potential solutions, or try to change your perspective.

In whatever manner you deem appropriate, take care of yourself. Establishing a period in your agenda to devote to your own requirements is of the utmost importance. The word "self-care" can be used to refer to a wide variety of activities that are beneficial to keeping one's mental and emotional health in good condition. with order to assist you with your day-to-day self-care, here are some suggestions.

You should get at least seven or eight hours of sleep every night; even 10 hours of sleep will cause you to feel sleepy.

While ingesting an adequate amount of protein and fiber, you should steer clear of sugar, processed foods, and alcohol.

Maintaining an aerobic heart rate can be accomplished by moving about frequently and stretching on a daily basis; ten thousand steps is a fantastic goal, but five thousand steps is a reasonable beginning point you can work toward. Make it a habit to give yourself some time to unwind each and every day. When you are working on a computer, for example, you should effort to avoid gazing at a screen for extended periods of time.

Create a daily schedule that allows you to engage in activities that bring you joy, such as reading a book or watching a television show. Spend time outside and take pleasure in what nature has to offer; doing so is an excellent way to unwind and obtain some vitamin D. Simply pressing play will provide you with some guidance on how to feel better. During this episode of the Mind Podcast, editor and clinical social worker Amy Morin, who is certified as a licensed clinical social worker, discusses a way for overcoming depression. Bring in a professional who specializes in mental health.

Is there something challenging going on in your life at the moment, or have you ever had to deal with a traumatic experience in the past? Are you concerned about a problem that may be related to your mental health? If this is the case, your best options would be to consult with a mental health expert who has received training in the field. Medication and talk therapy are two examples of successful treatments that are available for mental health issues. These treatments are offered for a variety of conditions, including anxiety, depression, and personality disorders. When used exactly as directed, medication has the potential to improve your mood and make it easier to put into practice the coping methods that you have acquired during treatment. It may be helpful to seek professional support from a therapist in order to enable introspection and modification of viewpoint.

Therapeutic and Counseling Services That Can Be Trusted The online counseling services that we have tested and assessed in an objective manner include Regain, Betterhelp, and Offered Online Talkspace, to name just a few of the best options available.
Have your issues addressed.

If you feel that you are suffering from anxiety, there are other options available to you besides consulting with a mental health expert. The following is a list of suggestions that are recommended.

If you have trouble relaxing, you might want to try taking an Ashwagandha supplement. Researchers have demonstrated that this plant has the potential to be beneficial in the treatment of a wide range of neurological conditions. 1. In the event that it is required, apply essential oils such as lavender oil.

Employing progressive muscle relaxation or another relaxation technique (PMR) is an effective method for relieving stress. You should put down the phone and take a break from social media and the news for a bit. By reading books or listening to podcasts, you can get some expert guidance on how to control your anxiety and reduce its symptoms. Regularly engage in some mild stretching, yoga, or brisk walking to improve your flexibility.

Be in charge of your mood, which is bipolar. But what if you always feel like you're in a bad mood? For those who are uncertain about whether medication or treatment would be beneficial, it is best to seek the advice of a competent mental health professional. For some people, the fogginess that comes along with depression can lead them to believe that aid is pointless or that other people have it worse than they do, which would lead them to believe that they do not deserve support.

In the event that this is the case, you ought to discuss how you are feeling with another man or woman. If you give them a call, you can inquire about the possibility of scheduling an appointment with the physician.

Although it is always an option to seek the assistance of a professional, there are strategies that you may implement on your own to reduce the symptoms of depression.

Because of the well-established depressive effects of alcohol, it is recommended that individuals who are experiencing depression abstain from drinking it.

Maintain your fitness routine; doing so will cause the release of endorphins, which may provide some relief in the short term.

Maintain a consistent sleep schedule; studies have shown that feelings of depression can be caused by both an excessive amount of sleep and an insufficient amount of sleep.

Reconsider your negative assumptions and assumptions: It would be beneficial for you to get a self-help book on cognitive behavioral therapy (CBT) for depression so that you can achieve your goals.

Improve yourself on a daily basis. In the event that you are having difficulty getting started, it is advisable to begin with smaller, more manageable steps in order to gain momentum for greater ones.

Take notes about your feelings on a daily basis: If you could, please write a list of everything that causes you stress on a daily basis and assign a score of ten to each of those items. Maintaining a journal of your joy will serve you well in the long run. A record of all of your accomplishments and the benefits that have been bestowed upon you should be kept.

Do not hold on to your misery. Despite the fact that there is a predetermined standard that each of us need to strive to accomplish, the reality is that no one is ever content with their life exactly as it is. On a daily and yearly basis, each and every one of us will go through periods of our lives that are comparable to highs and lows.

It is possible that it would be more advantageous for you to allow yourself to remain unhappy for a period of time if you are unable to identify the specific cause of your melancholy feeling.

When you are dealing with challenges related to your mental health, you should never turn a blind eye to the situation. It's possible that you find yourself in disagreement with the notion that everyone deserves to be happy all the time on a consistent basis.

Just keep in mind that you will eventually triumph over the difficulties you are facing, regardless of how awful they grow. Surprisingly, you could experience a sense of relief when you come to terms with the reality of your experiences and give up on the pursuit of happiness that lasts forever.

Methods for the management of emotions that are not entirely clear: Actions to take when everything appears to be in order.

In situations where everything seems to be going swimmingly, it may be more difficult to find an answer to the question "what's wrong with me?" during those times. Why do you feel that way if everything seems to be in order from the outside? What could be the reason for your feelings? More than simply depression or another mental health condition could be influencing your emotional state. There are other potential factors as well.

The following is a list of potential explanations for this:
It's possible that you put the needs of other people ahead of your own, which results in you failing miserably to portray yourself as genuine. You might start to feel remorse about your career choice if the role you are now in does not provide you with sufficient challenges.

As a result of your successful completion of a key objective, you could be wondering what the next step is. There is a possibility that you are ready for a change since you are tired of being in the same place.

If you are experiencing feelings of unhappiness, it is likely due to the absence of one of these items in your life. Due to the fact that an outsider would presume that everything is going well for you, this is typically the most challenging issue to handle. On the other side, regardless of how bad things go in your life, you can still feel like you have a lot of room for improvement. Keeping a notebook can be a useful tool for more in-depth research and analysis of such intricate feelings so that one can better understand them. Particularly in the event that there is not an immediate requirement for treatment as a result of a mental health emergency.

Find out what will make you happy before you put pen to paper by being curious and finding out what will inspire you. Continue to request clarification until you are provided with answers. If there are certain feelings that you don't really allow yourself to experience very often, free writing is an excellent way to get in touch with those feelings again. This is what Verywell means.

If you are unable to remove the idea that there is something wrong with you, you will be at a loss for what steps to take in order to better yourself. It is common practice to begin the process of deciding the subsequent course of action by first identifying the origin of your feelings. Do you feel like your health is failing you in some way? At that point, it is highly recommended that you schedule a consultation with your local physician. It's possible that the opposite is also true if you have a mental illness. As a result of the excessive amount of pressure that you are experiencing, do you believe that there is anything wrong with your life? The best course of action would be to figure out how to reduce the strain you are experiencing and make the most of the situation you are now in.

It may be the most difficult element of the process to discover a remedy when you are unsure of what the problem is. Take a break from the conversation and focus on what your thoughts are trying to tell you. You will be better ready to start making changes in your life once you have gained an awareness of thought patterns and after you have learned how to adjust your thinking in order to experience the outcomes that you truly desire.

In conclusion, it is imperative that you seek assistance if you are experiencing difficulties and nothing seems to be going in the right direction. It is important to remember that we are all flawed; if you are having trouble making sense of your life, please know that you have support from other people who understand and are prepared to listen to you while you work through your problems. forward with a positive outlook.

13 of the most effective strategies to change your point of view:

How you interpret the world around you is directly proportional to the perspective you have. Maintaining a gloomy view can have negative consequences for a variety of aspects of your life, including your work, your relationships, and your health. On top of that, studies have demonstrated that pessimism can be a self-sustaining characteristic, which can result in an unending cycle.

The good news is that we can improve our cognitive capacities by consistently practicing a few simple procedures. As part of their membership in the Forbes Coaches Council, the coaches have offered the following recommendations.
Every one of the thirteen mentors discusses the ways in which they overcame negative mental habits in this essay.

Every day, take some time for yourself to rest. By focusing on negative thoughts for ten minutes each day, you can instead learn to control them and learn to control them. Negative Thought Time

(NTT) should be scheduled for ten minutes that are set aside each day. In the event that you find yourself ruminating on unfavorable thoughts during the day, jot them down and make a commitment to revisit them during your time off. In due time, you will be able to overcome your pessimistic view and get control of the scenario through which you find yourself.

Changing your negative lens is the second step. Let's forget about the term "overcoming"; the term "replacing" refers to the process of reestablishing mental processes that are more useful. Negative thought patterns are pervasive, much like well-traveled roads in our minds, and they are everywhere. Directions that are easy to understand.

Locating the point at which the trend initially began is the first step. The second stage is to recognize when you have reached a plateau and be ready to make adjustments because you are ready to make changes.

Be as explicit as possible about the modifications that you would want to see in the third paragraph. Take a completely new option that will get you one step closer to achieving your goals.

In the third place, you should strive to be your own best friend.

Humans have a tendency to be somewhat critical of themselves. A great deal of what we say to ourselves is quite important. Following these simple steps will get you started:

Simply put it in there. 1. Letting go of it will allow you to stop dwelling on it and begin living your life. Within the next three minutes, we will put an end to this period of self-pity.

It is important to pay attention to it and to remain vigilant. Acquire the ability to recognize negative ideas. Reevaluation will be possible as a result of new understanding.

Finally, give it a new form. Now that you understand the reasons for your harsh behavior, you should make effort to place yourself in the position of your closest friend and listen to what they would say. Next, you need reassure yourself that you are worthy of this. 4. Make a note of it if you are unsure about it. It is important to pay attention to the origin of the negative attitude. Putting a notion that is disagreeable or confusing down on paper makes it much simpler to absorb and get past what is being spoken. Find out what you like, what you love, and what you are grateful for, and make effort to learn them.

Maintain a good frame of mind regarding both your thoughts and activities. Whether you do so verbally or in silence, expressing your gratitude, happiness, and love for the things that you have in your life is an effective method. Are you ready to take part in a discussion that takes a deep dive? Today's coffee is very delectable."This chair is comfortable enough for my back."I am thankful that I was given the opportunity to discuss our thoughts with my group. Solace is always close by, even when we are feeling low. If you simply make the decision to actively seek it out, it will be available to you. This is Wendy Pitts Reeves, a consultant with PLLC.

The Forbes Coaches Council is a group that is inaccessible to the general public and is comprised of the most renowned business and career coaches. Could I take part in this?

Be truthful with yourself and ask yourself things that are difficult.

Consider how you respond to demands that are difficult to fulfill. How can one possibly benefit from constantly focusing on the bad aspects of a situation? From this, what am I going to be able to salvage? In the event that I allow my negative thoughts to take control, what am I going to lose? In the event that this is the case, what is the cost? As a third question, how can I profit from adopting a positive mindset? Is there a price to pay for adopting a more optimistic point of view? For what reason do I always choose to look at things from a negative perspective?

Form new routines and routines

Rather than "overcoming" negative thought patterns, it is more productive to reframe the process as the creation of new habits. This is a more constructive way of looking at things. You are able to accomplish this by focusing your attention on things that you already have a positive attitude toward, which will result in your thoughts on those things being more upbeat. It might be anything from going to the beach to spending time with a pet that you adore spending time with. Let's begin with something simple, shall we?

Do not listen to the news in the morning.

According to studies, the risk of having an unpleasant day is significantly increased when one is exposed to terrible news, even if it is only for three minutes first thing in the morning. According to research, having a positive mindset can increase productivity, enjoyment at work, and it can also reduce the number of errors that occur. It is possible to alter the mental state of another person, but doing so is not always an easy task. To avoid feeling down, you should avoid viewing the morning news or anything else that could potentially bring you down.

Make use of statements that are affirmative.

At the moment that you open your eyes in the morning, you should express gratitude to God because it is a fresh day. If you want to get your day off to a good start, try jotting down some positive comments about yourself. Some examples of such phrases include "I love the people I work with," "I make positive contributions every day," and "I'm open to inspired thought." In the event that you ever find yourself questioning your capabilities, simply go back to a time when you overcame a challenge and had a sense of accomplishment. Maintaining a positive mindset requires effort on a daily basis, but it is well worth the effort once it is achieved.

Establish a framework that will ensure your success.

A routine that I have referred to as "Quantum Programming" has been a part of my morning routine for the past fifteen years since I began it. Take some time first thing in the morning to reflect on the things you want to accomplish in your life and the kind of person you want to become. This is an essential component of this practice. In the process of working toward the accomplishment of your long-term goals, you have also established a number of significant benchmarks. Whenever you decide to do something for yourself and put in a lot of effort to make it happen, negativity disappears.

Channel your energies toward a project that will be beneficial to the world.

Identifying the pattern of negative thought and establishing a goal that is both positive and inspiring is an excellent (and successful) strategy to combat negative thought habits. As a consequence of this, make a decision to spare yourself from worrying about evil for a period of five minutes whenever you find yourself doing so. This is something that I have recently finished, and it has caused an entirely new company to move forward at a fast speed.

There is a common tendency to underestimate the relevance of appreciation to one's happiness. In spite of the fact that life is not becoming any simpler, we can become more resilient by recasting the difficulties in light of all the positive moments that occur in our regular lives. Construct a useful list, and make sure to consult it frequently. It is important to be as specific as possible and to focus on what it is that you truly desire. It is possible to achieve success over the long run by maintaining a positive attitude and a clear mind.

Try out some different approaches for movement meditation.

As someone who has worked as a yoga instructor, a writing coach, and an author, I can say from personal experience that if you want to rid your mind of negative thoughts, you need to take action. If you want to break free of your thoughts that are overly theoretical, you need to bring your focus back to your physical self. Simply engaging in a brief session of yoga or focused breathing exercises (a sitting meditation that lasts for ten to fifteen minutes) is all that is required to disrupt these mental habits. Your ability to concentrate will improve if you incorporate some physical activity into your daily routine.

Getting rid of concepts that are pointless: a guide

Negative thinking can make a variety of issues, such as social anxiety, melancholy, stress, and low self-esteem, significantly more difficult to manage. The first step toward altering your current thought pattern is to become aware of the effects it has on your life and the issues it produces.

The way we think has an effect on how we feel and the actions that we take. In spite of the fact that we all have random, unproductive thoughts from time to time, it is essential to be ready to deal with these ideas when they appear in order to prevent them from derailing our day. The following explanation is provided by Rachel Goldman, a clinical assistant professor at the New York University School of Medicine and a psychologist. Changes in one's thinking patterns are something that can be accomplished by anyone on their own, despite the fact that talking to a therapist can be helpful for multiple situations. In this section, we will discuss a few of the strategies that you could take in order to change your negative attitude. Your goal should be to maintain a state of mind that is fully present and mindful at all times. Through the practice of meditation, the idea of awareness was initially conceived. If one want to engage in the practice of mindfulness, they must first acquire the ability to disengage from their own internal experiences and examine their own thoughts and feelings with the impartiality of a scientist. One method for increasing one's self-awareness is to engage in the practice of mindfulness, which involves concentrating on the present moment.

The ultimate goal of mindfulness training is to bring about a change in the way an individual interacts with their own thoughts.

When it comes to dealing with your internal monologue, the most successful method is to think of it as a series of items that you may either pause and observe or simply let float. Be conscious of the fact that your ideas are the source of your feelings and the behaviors you engage in. Take a look at the thoughts that you have. Put in the effort to ascertain the degree to which this idea may be implemented. Exactly what are you hoping to accomplish by adopting this way of thought into practice? The more you think about something, the more feelings come up inside of you.

The goal of mindfulness training is to retrain the rational brain, which is responsible for controlling emotional responses. According to the recommendations of a number of psychologists, practicing mindfulness, which can be defined as being fully present in the here and now, can help you make better use of your ideas.

Mindfulness may be able to lessen the impact of negative thinking, according to the findings of a study that found that practitioners of mindfulness reported having fewer negative thoughts in response to unfavorable imagery.

- The anti-anxiety effects of practicing mindfulness meditation

Your thoughts contain concepts that are not productive. While you are training yourself to recognize and classify negative thinking patterns and cognitive distortions, it is important to keep a close eye on your internal monologue. One example of "black and white thinking" is when an individual has a self-image that is either fully good or completely negative, regardless of the external variables that influence them. The following is an extra collection of examples that illustrate undesirable mental processes: This category of cognitive error is characterized by the erroneous projection of future events or the extrapolation of thoughts that have been expressed by other individuals.

It is possible that you are suffering from catastrophicism, which is a form of pessimism, if you are always experiencing anxiety about the worst possible outcome, regardless of whether there are alternatives that are better or more acceptable.

One of the characteristics of the overgeneralization paradigm is the tendency to tend to generalize the results of a single experiment to all of the possible possibilities. When you let yourself believe that terrible things are going to happen, your life might become even more stressful and gloomy than it really is. It is possible for a person's self-esteem to be negatively affected by negative self-labeling in a variety of different settings. If, for example, you are able to persuade yourself that you are "bad at math," you could make effort to avoid activities that need your mathematical ability. An viewpoint that is pessimistic is characterized by thinking that is too preoccupied with what one "should" do. Due to the fact that these assertions are not within the realm of possibility, the audience members are left feeling disheartened and discouraged about their chances of achieving their goals.

When you make a belief about something based on your thoughts about it rather than on evidence, you are engaging in emotional reasoning with yourself. Anxieties are strong emotions, and it is simple to allow them to convince you that your well-being is in danger just because you are experiencing them. One of the potential outcomes is an intensification of worry as well as other unfavorable emotions.

This school of thought places a significant emphasis on attributing significance or blame to external factors when the true perpetrators are found within the organization. It is for this reason that a great number of people accuse themselves of being responsible for things that they were unable to alter.

Patterns of thought that are distracting are classified according to the tiny distinctions between them. The use of irrational reasoning and assumptions that are not grounded in reality is the common thread that runs through all of them.

According to Goldman, this is the stage in which you need to recognize the beliefs that are detrimental to you. Now that you are aware of the concept, you are able to recognize it for what it truly is: a damaging thought, similar to an all-or-nothing thinking or a cognitive distortion. Create a mental note of it and give it a name. Recall it later. The fact that it "infers" anything is shown by this.

An additional piece of advice is to pause for a moment and acknowledge the concept for what it actually is. It is important to keep in mind that this is merely a working hypothesis and not a proven reality.

Negative thinking can originate from a wide variety of sources, and incorrect reasoning is just one of them. A reduction in the impact of these fallacies can be achieved by first acknowledging their existence and then keeping in mind that our beliefs do not correspond to reality. You should make an effort to steer clear of particular modes of thinking if you suffer from seasonal affective disorder.

Instead of thinking negative thoughts, try thinking positive ones:

Cognitive restructuring is an integral component of each and every cognitive behavioral therapy (CBT) program. Through the application of these strategies, you will be able to recognize thoughts that are not constructive and replace them with thoughts that are more effective. Cognitive restructuring is a procedure that involves detecting negative thoughts, examining these thoughts to ensure that they are accurate, and then changing them. You can engage in cognitive restructuring either in therapy or on your own.

In his suggestion, Goldman says that one should examine the arguments both in favor of and against the idea. It could prompt you to rethink your assumptions and come up with answers that are superior and more applicable to the situation. The ability to think in a positive and rational manner will become instinctive with practice and time, despite the fact that it will initially be difficult. It is possible to modify one's thinking by going through the stages of cognitive restructuring that are as follows:

Make certain that the proposal is feasible. Evaluate the validity of your current beliefs by considering what has occurred in the past in conditions that are comparable to those that you are currently experiencing.

You should give it a lot of thought and to find any potential problems with it. Take the time to carefully weigh the benefits and drawbacks of continuing to have trust in the concept. Catastrophizing is a cognitive distortion that everyone should be aware of. It is crucial to be aware of it.

Conduct an analysis of your thoughts and think about the advice you would provide to a friend who shared them with one another. Research conducted by Johns Hopkins Medicine suggests that persons who are coping with depression should to concentrate on more positive aspects of their lives. Ascertain whether there is any positive aspect to the situation that you are currently facing. On the other side, Goldman cautions against substituting data that are negative with ones that are overly optimistic. In order for these "alternative concepts" to be successful, they need to be grounded in reality. In order to avoid thinking, it is not a good idea to substitute an option that is not feasible. If you find yourself in a similar circumstance, it might be beneficial to ask yourself what you would say to a buddy.

In the event that you constantly tell yourself things such as "I'm a failure" or "I'm going to fail," Goldman advises that you should not attempt to convince yourself otherwise. In its place, you should try telling yourself things like, "I am confident that I will be successful."

The alternative that she offers is to say something along the lines of "I'm not sure I can do this, but I'm trying my best," which is a remark that is more neutral and self-compassionate.

A single session of cognitive restructuring is all that is required for individuals to overcome the biases and negative attitudes that are the root cause of anxiety, according to research. Be sure to tune in to Verywell Mind for sensible advice from professionals working in the field. The act of making a decision should not be delayed.

In contrast to this, mental suppression is what you have when you practice mindfulness. The method requires actively seeking out and rejecting any negative mental processes that may be present.

Regardless of how much you try to push away negative ideas, they will eventually come back to haunt you. The "reflection" process is the name given to this kind of accomplishment. The most effective method is to practice mindfulness, which reduces the influence of your thoughts and makes them less significant in general.

They believe that it is much more distressing when bad thoughts come back to you after you have made an effort to repress them. However, researchers in the field of psychology often advise that you should take action in order to combat negative ideas.

When you repress your ideas, you end up making yourself more worried in the long run, even though it could be helpful in the short term. If you do things on your own, you will learn how to deal with criticism.

CBT, which stands for cognitive behavioral therapy, includes a component called "assertive self-advocacy," which may also be beneficial for individuals who suffer from social anxiety. In light of the fact that you will invariably come into contact with people who are quite critical of you at times, it is essential that you have the ability to deal with criticism and rejection.

An example of a typical therapeutic activity is acting out a conversation with your therapist. There is an opportunity for you to practice being more aggressive and offering feedback that is helpful during this time. One of the most important aspects of homework is for students to put what they have learned in class into practice in the real world.

In order to better deal with challenging circumstances, such as receiving criticism, you can find it helpful to have the ability to respond aggressively in advance. The fact that encounters in the real world can provide opportunities to put this technique into action is another factor that is taken into consideration while developing this method.

Furthermore, a number of studies have demonstrated that it is advantageous to address "social mistakes," which are known to enhance anxiety and negative thoughts.

If you want to be able to deal with the negative thoughts that come into your head when you are subjected to criticism or rejection, improving your ability to bounce back from unsuccessful situations can be of great assistance. Your capacity for resilience can be improved if you acquire the ability to bear the worry that these events occasionally bring about.

Develop a habit of keeping a journal on a regular basis.
Keeping a "thought diary" or journal of one's thoughts is one method that can be utilized in order to gain control over harmful thought patterns. Keep a thought journal if you want to learn how to regulate your ideas and stop responding emotionally to random events. This might be a beneficial tool for you if you want to take control of your thoughts.

When participating in cognitive behavioral therapy (CBT), one of the activities that is commonly done is keeping a notebook of thoughts. It is possible that keeping a thought journal could be an effective method for processing negative thoughts and feelings associated to a date, for example. In the event that you are interested in transforming your destructive and pessimistic perspective on rejection into one that is more constructive and constructive, this study will demonstrate how to accomplish this.

What are some ways that keeping a mental notebook could be helpful for someone who suffers from social anxiety?

Having said that, let's begin by defining what negative thinking is. Any perception of oneself, one's circumstances, or the actions of another that is influenced by bias is considered to be a bad notion. They have been linked to a number of mental health problems, including mood disorders, among other things. Just a few of the more common ones are as follows: 9) "I'll never be good enough". "They must think I'm stupid for saying that", together with the statement "This situation is bound to get ugly."

My thoughts are constantly pessimistic, and I have no idea why that is the case. It's not abnormal to have a negative attitude on life. People who have a negativity bias tend to give more weight to negative influences than they do to good ones, which can result in pessimistic thinking emerging. Consider the possibility that, from an evolutionary point of view, it was more advantageous for the species to have a pessimistic outlook. ten It is possible for cognitive distortions to be the cause of negative thinking. Characteristics like this are present in a number of the symptoms of anxiety and depression.

This should urge you to seek the advice of a mental health expert, according to someone interpretation, which states that "if you discover that persistent negative thoughts are negatively impacting your life," you should seek their assistance. It might be difficult to entrust another individual with sensitive information; nevertheless, therapists are equipped with the abilities necessary to recognize unhealthy thought patterns and assist patients in replacing them with more beneficial alternatives.

The difficulty of retraining his clients' minds to think in a more hopeful manner is something that Goldman emphasizes to his clients on a consistent basis. She claims that it is possible to replace negative automatic thoughts with more positive ones with the application of time and effort, despite the fact that it may be difficult at first. The Reasons Behind Delaying Stress Relief and the Possible Solutions to This Problem One of the most common forms of procrastination is the act of delaying important decisions or obligatory tasks. Procrastination is defined as the act of delaying the commencement of a task until the very last minute, even if the individual had intended to begin the task earlier. According to research, twenty percent of adults and fifty percent of students are affected by it on a regular basis.

Mental tension, which can arise from either within or outside the individual, is one of the key reasons for the multiple bad results that can be attributed to procrastination. As a result of the inverse relationship that exists between stress and procrastination, the stress-procrastination loop is quite prevalent among chronic procrastinators.

Therefore, it is beneficial to have an understanding of the whys and hows of their interaction in order to provide relief from tension and procrastination. The purpose of this essay is to provide you with assistance in your endeavor by analyzing the relationship between stress and procrastination and providing guidance on how to deal with both of these issues.

A correlational investigation on the relationship between work deferral and psychological distress If you want to prevent tension, put things off till next time. The consequences that result from delaying tasks till a later time Relax and put off doing housework for a while.

What are the consequences of putting off tasks? Putting things off until later creates stress in two primary ways, which are as follows:

In the long run, procrastination will result in a large amount of distress because of its cumulative effect. Procrastination can have a bad impact on mental health in a number of ways. One of these ways is that it can cause people to feel nervous because they are concerned that they will not have sufficient time to complete the task at hand. People frequently put things off as a typical response to the pressure that they are under. When a person is under too much pressure to concentrate on the task at hand, they may choose to procrastinate by engaging in something insignificant, such as scrolling through social media.

For instance, if a person experiences stress as a result of procrastination but does not experience any subsequent procrastination as a result of stress is an example of a one-sided relationship that may be experienced by certain individuals. Unfortuitously, there are instances in which individuals erroneously assume that this link operates in both directions, which can result in a vicious cycle of stress and procrastination.

Either the person who procrastinates is unable to break out of this cycle, or they are motivated to complete the task by something that is external to oneself, such as a deadline. On the other hand, the stress-procrastination cycle may be reignited with the procrastinator experiencing setbacks, such as experiencing feelings of being overwhelmed by a new job.

Remember that everyone is different, and that stress and procrastination are different responses to different situations. This is the last but not the least important point to keep in mind. Generally speaking, stress causes people to put things off until later, but in certain circumstances, such as when they are scared about the repercussions, it might actually cause them to act more quickly. This has significant ramifications because stress induces individuals to put things off until later.

If you want to prevent tension, put things off till next time. In certain circumstances, delaying the completion of tasks until a later period may, at the very least momentarily, have the opposite impact and alleviate tension. Let's say, for example, that a student's anxiety levels increase everytime he thinks about his next school project, but they decrease whenever he uses some form of internet procrastination to put it off till the very last minute before the deadline. Some people, whether they are aware of it or not, use delaying as a form of emotional regulation in order to lessen the amount of stress they are experiencing. In spite of the fact that it seems like a harmless technique to release stress, this kind of behavior is often considered to be maladaptive because it impedes progress toward one's goals. It is possible for a person's stress levels to increase when they start paying attention to their work for a variety of reasons, some of which may include the following. put on hold:

Take no action while you are ruminating on the current topic at hand. Doing a task in a short amount of time because you are under a great deal of time pressure. The experience of negative feelings, such as guilt, as a result of delaying the completion of tasks. The consequences of delaying responses, such as misunderstandings in communication.

Therefore, putting things off till later in the aim of lowering immediate tension is typically a waste of time because all it does is wait for the stress to actually begin, which means that the person who procrastinates "borrows" some time to feel better. a loan with a short repayment period that will result in interest payments from him when he pays it back. If the person who engages in procrastination is content to put things off until they are really necessary, or at the very least until their due dates have passed, then there is no reason to express concern regarding them. It is possible that the procrastinator will experience reduced stress as a consequence of this practice; but, they may also acquire additional issues, such as a continuing fight to achieve their goals. The consequences that result from delaying tasks till a later time.

There are a number of negative repercussions that are related with procrastination, including negative effects on mental and physical health, reduced quality of sleep, decreased financial stability, diminished interpersonal ties, decreased academic achievement, and general well-being.

To name just two of the many unfavorable results that might result from the stress that procrastination generates, mental and physical health problems are just two of the many potential outcomes. It is possible that the stress that is caused by procrastination could make existing illnesses and other physical health problems even more severe. Relax and put off doing housework for a while. By employing strategies for stress and procrastination, you can do more and feel better at the same time. Inquiry-based stress reduction is one strategy that can be followed. In a nutshell, the questions that are presented below can be of assistance to you in putting this strategy into action the next time you encounter an idea that causes you concern.

Will this idea continue to hold water? To what extent do you believe that this idea is reasonable?
Next, you will need to determine the origin of the stressful idea and the consequences that it brought about as a consequence of its existence. The following questions should be taken into consideration if you require assistance with this assignment.
What is the best way to deal with a scenario like this?
Is this causing you to feel relaxed or more anxious than you were before?

Whenever you think about this, what sorts of images from the past or the present come to mind for you?

How do you feel at that very moment, especially while you are thinking in such way?

When you think about something, feelings come to mind from that thought.

Do you find yourself thinking about compulsions or addictions as a result of it?

What kind of implications does this idea have for the way you interact with other people? In situations such as this, how can you ensure that you give yourself enough time to unwind and refresh yourself?

The second step is to imagine how you would feel if that worrisome concept were not there in your life and then to live in a world that is not skewed by it.

The question is, what are you if you do not possess that?

Last but not least, it is of the utmost importance to collect evidence that contradicts stressful thinking and to evaluate the chance that this conflicting argument is correct. For example, rather than thinking, "I won't be able to study well for the test," try thinking, "I'll be able to study well for the test." This will help you better prepare for the test. Following that, you should look for evidence that supports your new, more hopeful belief.

In addition, you have access to a wide variety of additional helpful strategies that can assist you in managing stress and inhibiting your tendency to put things off till later. Specifically, it is possible to do the following:

The task can be finished by breaking it down into smaller, more manageable portions. If, for instance, you find yourself unable to move past the first paragraph of a large research paper, you might want to consider breaking it up into smaller, more manageable sections.

Beginning with baby steps is the best way to get started. For those who have trouble getting started, you could try writing a single line or working out for two minutes. Once you have completed any of these activities, you should convince yourself that it is alright to stop. You are able to learn and improve from your mistakes if you give yourself permission to make them. Remember that your initial draft of an article, for example, is generally not going to be excellent. This is something you should expect. An important first step toward resolving your concerns is to acknowledge that you have them. Say to yourself, "Their opinion doesn't matter" if you are feeling nervous about reviews from a source that is not particularly important. Consider the future and make a strategy to deal with any and all potential outcomes. Consider the factors that could cause your work to be delayed, then devise a strategy to overcome those factors. Perform a smooth transition from one work to the next. Change gears and concentrate on something else until you are ready to tackle the first problem once more. For example, if you are stuck on a particular activity and can't seem to get over the initial obstacle, it is recommended that you switch gears and take a break from the activity. Organize your tasks in such a way that you will do them during the times when you are most productive. In order to get your day off to a good start, you should give yourself permission to be as creative as you possibly can.

Adapt the desktop to your likes. If, for example, you are having difficulties concentrating at your current job because of the background noise, you might want to consider wearing headphones that cancel out noise or looking for a location that is calmer.

Strengthening your social support system is something you should do. As an alternative, one might choose to surround themselves with positive influences that encourage them to develop while avoiding harmful effects. Another option is to select a person who is considered to be an authority figure or an exemplar to emulate. Your batteries need to be recharged as much as possible. There is a correlation between taking frequent pauses and preventing burnout when working on jobs that need a high level of focus. Remember that the short-term impacts of not getting enough sleep on your productivity are often more than compensated for by the long-term benefits to your health and productivity. This is something you should keep in mind if you want to maintain your motivation.

Work on developing your confidence in your abilities. You are confident in your own abilities and are aware that you are capable of achieving the goals that you have set for yourself. You may make it better in a number of different ways; one of them is to figure out how you are going to achieve your goals and then devise a strategy to work toward achieving them.

On the off chance that you have already put things off, you ought to give yourself some time off. In the event that you have failed to begin a task for an excessive amount of time, you should remind yourself, "I should not have put that off, but that is now in the past." At this point, what is most vital is to proceed with this endeavor. Do not give up. Discover how to treat oneself with kindness. To be more specific, you should work on developing the three pillars of self-compassion, which are self-benevolence (which means treating oneself kindly), common humanity (which means knowing that everyone has issues), and mindfulness (which means accepting your feelings without criticizing them).

The effort that you have put in will be acknowledged and appreciated. As an example, after a week of hard work studying, you can decide to reward yourself with a delectable snack. It is possible that determining the underlying causes of your anxiety and procrastination will assist you in selecting which of these tactics to implement. If you take this into consideration, you will be able to focus in on the tactics that are going to be most effective for you.

To add insult to injury, don't overlook the importance of making self-care a high priority by participating in activities such as regular exercise and sufficient relaxation. In addition, it is recommended that you seek the guidance of a skilled mental health expert if you have experienced significant stress or that you have also struggled with other major issues such as anxiety or depression.

In conclusion, it is important to keep in mind that although stress and procrastination are both issues, it may be more productive to look for solutions that target only one of these issues. Because of the interconnected nature of these issues, resolving one of them can have a positive impact on the others. For instance, if you are able to reduce the amount of time you spend procrastinating, you will experience a general reduction in the amount of stress you are experiencing.

To summarize, there are a variety of approaches to dealing with stress and procrastination; however, the next step is to determine the factors that are contributing to these issues. either this problem or that one. This category includes a variety of approaches, including but not limited to: inquiry-based stress reduction, work simplicity, baby steps, graceful failure, and appropriate sleep.

Method for Overcoming Obstacles and Being Successful in Achieving Your Objectives:

The obstacles that may prevent you from making progress toward your goals are referred to as. In order to make progress in life, it is necessary to conquer limitations, especially those that serve as obstacles to accomplishment.

You can only assert that you have achieved success in achieving these goals if you really carry them out. When you are right on the verge of passing away as a result of unanticipated losses and disappointments, life can be terribly unpleasant.

If we were to state that there are no challenges associated with any achievement, we would be misleading ourselves. The outcomes of these evaluations frequently reveal problems that call for attention to be paid to them. The degree of self-assurance you have in your capacity to achieve will be directly proportional to how well you are able to deal with these problems. There are seven arguments that justify their worth, which are the difficulties. Here is a concluding thought on the "Ways to

Overcome Obstacles in Life": advice that can be put into practice to overcome obstacles. The following is a list of seven of the many reasons why problems are particularly important.

In light of this, why is it essential to go through the process of suffering? What would it be like to live in a world where there are no boundaries? I will now present seven situations in which overcoming difficulties proved to be quite important.

Initially, there are a few challenges that should be anticipated. Exhibit your true nature and personality.

The challenges that you face in life have the potential to bring you to your knees. When you reach this point in your life, you will discover who you truly are. You could be surprised to discover that your genuine capabilities and habits are hiding from you at times. The goal of putting oneself in challenging circumstances is to force yourself out of your comfort zone so that you can grow and develop as a result of the experience. Learning to recognize both your strengths and weaknesses is a good way to start improving your chances of being successful. The completion of these tasks will disclose the true nature of your character.

Your response to challenges will determine whether you are successful or unsuccessful. The idea that one can walk on water if they know where to lay their rocks has received a lot of attention in the past. An innovative strategy can be designed as a response to the issues that you are now facing.

Consider this circumstance, in which someone wrongs you on a regular basis, as an opportunity to learn and engage in the practice of forgiveness. No matter what the issue is, there is always a method to solve it. A change in perspective is all that is required to get started on the path of gaining insight from hardship.

Not only that, but it is the reason! According to a quote attributed to Benjamin Franklin, "what does not kill you does not weaken yourself."

It is important to take the advice to heart, think about it, and then put it into behavior. Remember that adversity is what builds resilience, so keep that in mind. Resilience is not a quality that is innate to a person but rather a quality that can be taught. It is important to keep in mind that success will never come to you by chance. In the afterlife, this is the only time it is conceivable.

During your time here, you will be confronted with challenges and obstacles that you will need to conquer. A person's character and courage can be strengthened via the process of confronting adversity. It is possible that if you are dissatisfied with the way things are now going, it would be prudent to take a chance on a brighter future. Taking on a challenge could help you become more resilient so that you can confront the next level if you notice that your courage is beginning to wane.

The fact that you only have about two thousand weeks left to live is really insane, isn't it? There is a limited number of weeks in a lifetime; when you reach the age of 40, you will have around 2,000 weeks left.

Four challenges will help you hone in on what is most important to you. In order to fulfill your values, you need pay great attention to them and work hard to achieve them. Once you have a specific objective in sight, even the most daunting challenges will appear to be within your own control.

Every obstacle appears to be more difficult to overcome when you have no notion what you are trying to accomplish or where you are going.

If you want to be successful in overcoming the few problems that are worth your effort, you need to narrow your focus like a laser and have a clear grasp on your ultimate objectives.

Trials allow you to let your imagination flow, which is the sixth advantage of conducting them. In the event that you are involved in a head-on collision with a lion in the forest, your true running speed will be revealed. The splendor of life can be found in this very fact!

In the absence of obstacles, it is possible that you will not venture into uncharted territory. The vast majority of people are not motivated to study and do not possess the patience that is required for this endeavor. It is necessary to push yourself beyond your comfort zone and allow your creative side to peek through if you want to break free from limitations.

As we mentioned in point number six, when you are confronted with difficulties, you get a greater appreciation for the achievements you have already achieved.

Individuals will respond to you in a variety of ways depending on how you perceive them. Consider the actions taken by President Abraham Lincoln as an illustration. Lincoln was able to lead the United States of America through the Civil War with tremendous success, despite the fact that he struggled with depression.

Through his attempts to bring the nation together, Abraham Lincoln was able to triumph over his own personal challenges and discover a sense of purpose in his life. After some time, he became quite skilled at exercising patience. This concept was expressed by him, and he drew determination from adversity.

Because he discovered meaning and solace in something that was significant beyond himself, he was able to prevail over the challenges he faced. What your difficulties actually encompass and the means by which you can prevail over them There are seven obstacles that could lead you to a purpose that is higher than your own personal problems.
Moving away from self-pity and toward the enjoyment that you may bring to those around you is necessary in order to achieve the same level of contentment in life that Abraham Lincoln did. It is not uncommon to discover that the answer to overcoming one's own challenges is to assist other people in surmounting their own challenges.

This is one of the most effective methods for overcoming feelings of depression. The key to success with this strategy is to let go of your personal worries and concentrate on the pain of people who are in your immediate vicinity. Maintaining an exterior emphasis is beneficial to the process of inward development.

After you have gained an understanding of the value of obstacles, here are seven strategies to make the most of them.

- Identifying your challenges is the first step in the process.

Keep in mind the things that are holding you back from making progress. What is the extent to which these challenges are impeding your progress toward achieving your goals?

To what extent are you falling behind? The cause needs to be identified by you. Under no circumstances should you ever, ever, ever return to your list of complaints; doing so will only give you with further explanations instead. The phrase "I simply do not have time" should serve as a prompt for you to review the routine that you are currently following. You can be unable to make progress due to personal issues such as procrastination or environmental causes such as complacency when it comes to your advancement. "I don't have enough money" is typically near the top of the list of concerns that the majority of people have.

It is possible that you are experiencing difficulties at the moment owing to a lack of motivation, time, or both. There is also the possibility that you are aware that you need to concentrate on finding ways to increase your income while simultaneously minimizing your spending. Determine how many years this problem has been available to the public.

How long have you been coping with this issue? How long have you been dealing with it? I am curious as to what part of your habit or belief system you adhere to that is keeping you from achieving the goals you have set for yourself. It is necessary for you to have the answers to these questions in order to modify things in the appropriate manner.

In the event that you have just changed jobs, for instance, you can find that you are having difficulty with some aspects of your new job or workplace. This is due to the fact that you will be required to adapt to a different environment.

Keep in mind all of the challenges that you have overcome. Whether you choose to actively conquer your challenges or not, you can always learn from them and apply it to future attempts. This is true regardless of whether you want to actively conquer them or not.

- Give some thought to your existing position in relation to the universe.

It is not possible to achieve success in order to overcome every challenge. In their presence, you experience a sense of helplessness since they are so terrible. It's possible that you lack the strength to deal with challenging circumstances.

The repercussions of this shouldn't be considered disastrous. While you are doing this, take a few deep breaths and make a mental list of the things that you do, in fact, have control over. The amount of work that you put in is a model of behavior.
Your ability to decide whether or not to take an opportunity when it presents itself is fully under your hands.

A number of factors, including physical activity, diet, and leisure time, can have an effect on how you feel and behave.

Investigate the extent of your influence. As soon as possible, start working on developing as many desirable characteristics as you possibly can.

- In order to achieve success, you are required to.

The determination to keep going even when things get difficult is a more true description of a tremendous leap than any other type of leap. A comprehensive inventory of all the barriers that are preventing you from achieving your goals should be carried out, box by box. This is a smart course of action.

In the event that you have the objective of being the most accomplished copywriter on the entire planet, it is imperative that you enroll in a demanding online course. Participating in a writing course that is offered online can be a more practical option. If you instantly launch Google, you will be able to avoid this kind of problem.

- Insist on having a strategy in place.

Always be sure to work with a list of other tasks that need to be done. It is possible to get off to a good start for the day if you get things done early thing in the morning. Keeping in mind that there will be challenges and detours to overcome along the way. Through introspection and the application of lessons learned from past failures, you can enhance the goals and tactics you have for the future.

- Improve your ability to find solutions to difficulties.

Working on becoming more analytical is something you should do if you have a tendency to make decisions based on your gut instinct. In the event that you are still unable to decide on a plan of action, the following may be feasible: What steps would I take next if I decided to enroll in a writing class but ended up failing it? Developing a backup plan is a smart thing to do.

Consider both the positive and negative aspects of taking the writing class before making a decision. Find out if the benefits are more than the drawbacks in this situation.

- Take a look at how far you've come.

Maintain a notebook in which you record both your achievements and your failures as you work toward achieving your goals. Establish objectives, and you will be compensated after they are accomplished. To keep track of your progress, you have the option of doing one of the following four things.

- Not the least of the list.

The obstacles that we are able to conquer make life a better experience. For as long as you are human, you will undoubtedly face challenges. A positive mindset and a shift in perspective are two things that you need to accomplish in order to be successful in overcoming challenges. They can be used either as barriers or as stepping stones, depending on your preference. You have the ability to make a deliberate choice about the way you want to live your life and to put the guidance that I have offered above into practice in order to triumph over any challenges that may come your way. Make certain that you are robust and well-protected. Take control of your worst fears.

- Formulate a strategy for the future.

If you want any guidance, you should either confront your worries or try to escape them. The majority of people experience some level of anxiety. The primary defense mechanisms are activated when there is fear. It is possible that you will be able to abstain from engaging in a harmful activity if you are able to stop yourself in time. On the other hand, situations such as giving a public speech, which is not genuinely dangerous, may drive you to develop an anxiety that is not rightfully yours. A considerable fear of public speaking might hinder a person from participating in meaningful social and professional rituals. One example of this is the toasting of a close friend's wedding. This is just one example.

It's possible that you believe that your fear is preventing you from taking the plunge and traveling on that dream trip to Europe that you've always dreamed going on. If your fear is limiting you from living your life to the fullest or is leading to larger difficulties, confronting your fear head-on can teach you coping techniques and help you overcome it. Your fear may also be contributing to larger problems.

You shouldn't try to prevent yourself from dealing with your concerns; rather, you should figure out how to deal with them, consult a therapist, and perhaps even confront them head-on. If, on the other hand, your fear does not prevent you from living your life, you should probably stop and think about how necessary it is to confront it.

The potential risks should be identified and evaluated.

When individuals do not have sufficient knowledge about a topic, their anxiety levels may increase.

1. An illustration of this would be the fact that you can have a crippling fear of flying as a result of all the news articles that focus on awful accidents that take place in the air.

You will come to the conclusion that the probability of passing away on a commercial flight in the United States is not even close to being guaranteed if you do the math. The odds are one in seven million, which is significantly lower than the odds of smoking, which are one in 600. When you are properly secured in your seat, turbulence does not pose a significant hazard to you, and the jolts and jolts that you experience when flying have a rational meaning. For less palpable worries, such as anxiety about public speaking, quantifiable data may not always be able to adequately convey the situation. You can improve your self-assurance by reading about the experiences of other people who have been public speakers or by researching practices that have been successful.

When you avoid something, it does not mean that you should do it simply because it makes you feel uncomfortable. In order to gain an understanding of the potential dangers and the gravity of the situation, you will need to engage in activities that cause you to feel fear. Formulate a strategy for the future. It takes baby steps that are consistent in order to conquer your worries. Making an attempt to carry out a dangerous activity before you are prepared to do so can result in absolutely devastating outcomes.

Maintain a forward momentum at all times, on the other hand. It is totally normal to experience anxiousness to a moderate degree. It is possible that you will squander a significant amount of time waiting for nothing to occur if you wait for your fear to subside before taking action.

It is best to break down your worries into smaller, more manageable chunks and work your way up to the larger ones. This will allow you to maximize your efficiency. The following are some of the ways that exposure therapy can be utilized to assist individuals in overcoming their fear of using public speaking:

Practicing your pitch in front of a mirror for just two minutes will help you feel more confident.

After you have finished listening to the recording of your chat, you should evaluate how well you performed.
Rehearse with a friend how to respond to the particular circumstance.

The best way to acquire a sense of it is to discuss it with someone you can rely on. For the purpose of practicing the speech, you should get yourself, a member of your immediate family, and one of your friends together. Your speech should be practiced in front of two friends, your spouse, and a member of your own personal family. The presentation should be made during a meeting with the company members. As a potential treatment option, virtual reality (VR) exposure therapy may be considered in certain circumstances. Evidence suggests that there is a treatment that is beneficial for post-traumatic stress disorder (also known as PTSD). Seek the guidance of an experienced individual. It is suggested that you seek the advice of a licensed mental health professional if you are experiencing symptoms of a medical condition such as an eating disorder, social anxiety disorder, or post-traumatic stress disorder, or if your fears are causing you to experience difficulties in your day-to-day life experiences. Certain individuals who suffer from specific phobias, a form of persistent anxiety disorder, may experience a sense of helplessness when confronted with their concerns.

With the assistance of a cognitive behavioral therapist, you will be able to educate yourself on how to control your anxiety. Patients suffering from a wide variety of phobias, such as stage fright and arachnophobia, have been patients that the majority of mental health therapists have previously worked with. Confronting your anxieties head-on is not an easy task; however, therapy can be of assistance by providing you with a secure environment in which to discuss them and by teaching you strategies to deal with them. With the assistance of a therapist, you will be able to make progress at a pace that is both controlled and beneficial.

Acceptance and Commitment treatment (ACT) is one component of fear-based treatment that may be taken into consideration. Through this approach, you will learn to embrace your concerns and establish a commitment to making them more manageable. Experiential learning, which can also be referred to as "immersion" or "exposure" therapy, is characterized by the following: it involves the repetition of stressful events, which is essential to exposure therapy, which is designed to assist individuals in overcoming phobias.

Concepts from psychoanalysis:

One of the fundamental objectives of psychoanalytic treatment for phobias and terror is to identify and eradicate the underlying cause of the psychological condition being treated.

Dealing with Fear: Methods and Techniques In spite of the fact that postponing your worries would make you feel better in the present moment, it may wind up making your worry far worse in the future. The amygdala, which is the part of the brain that is responsible for fear, is aware of the fact that ignoring your concerns will not enhance your ability to deal with them. Nevertheless, you can minimize your anxiety by "acclimating" your amygdala, which means teaching your brain to handle fear. You can do this by confronting your anxieties gradually, in little doses that do not overwhelm you.

According to the findings of an animal study that was published in Science, the brain needs to be repeatedly exposed to fear in order for it to be able to overcome it. Rats and mice were slightly shocked by researchers while they were confined in a cage. Following that, they continue to maintain the same rats in a cage for an extended period of time without shocking them. In the beginning, the mice did not respond to it, but after being subjected to it on many occasions, they gradually ceased doing so.

In spite of the fact that the findings of studies conducted on animals cannot be transferred to human subjects, the concept of "facing your fears" nevertheless aims to accomplish the same thing. Consider the possibility that it is time to face your fears.

You don't have to put any pressure on yourself to conquer any worries that you might have. If you live far enough inland, your fear of tsunamis might not have a significant impact on your day-to-day life like you might think. On the other hand, this may become a problem for you if you live in close proximity to the ocean and experience a great deal of anxiety whenever there are reports of storms, earthquakes, or high tides, or if you choose not to go on vacation. It is something that you would generally select since you would prefer to be in a location that is not in close proximity to the water.

Address your phobias by having a conversation with yourself about the ways in which they are hindering you from going forward. Are you of the opinion that the challenges you face hinder you from enjoying the life you had envisioned for yourself?

Consider both the benefits and the drawbacks of confronting your fear. The documentation of them is absolutely necessary. Examine the advantages of addressing your concerns head-on in comparison to the disadvantages of doing so. You should make a list of all the positive things that will occur if you are successful in overcoming your concerns.

Look at the information that has been gathered if you want to know what the next step is.

Fear versus phobia:

It is helpful to have an understanding of the distinction between a common fear and a phobia before making the decision to address your fear single-handedly. Psychologists are in agreement that the defining elements of a phobia are the degree to which the fear reaction is severe and the degree to which the phobia affects the individual's day-to-day functioning.

It is also possible to watch jets take off and land from an airport that is located nearby, or you could simply park your car and take in the beauty. For those who wish to overcome their phobia of airplanes, conducting research on the subject and gaining first-hand experience could be beneficial. In the event that you believe you are unable to deal with a frightening circumstance, you can attempt practicing how to deal with it through the use of imaginary exposure. To illustrate the idea, it is not easy to place oneself in the position of another person and generate the courage to board an airplane or other kind of transportation. Put yourself in the pilot's seat and imagine that you are witnessing takeoff for the very first time. Phobias are mental illnesses that drive people to worry more than is necessary in response to actual dangers, whereas anxieties are a normal and expected part of being human. Take for example the fear of flying, often known as aerophobia. If you are frightened of flying, you can choose to forgo traveling completely or look for other means to get where you need to go. Beliefs and concerns regarding theft, especially in circumstances when there is no intention to steal For the purpose of avoiding airports I feel an increasing amount of anxiety each time an airplane passes over my location. At some point, you will either be unable to board the plane at all, or you will experience a significant physical reaction such as shaking, sweating, or sobbing throughout the entire flight. There are a number of therapeutic alternatives available to those who suffer from phobias. These include medication, guided therapy, and other ways that enable patients to confront their anxieties. Patients can find relief from their phobias through these treatment options. Confronting a phobia head-on is the most effective method for overcoming it; nevertheless, it is imperative that you do it in a safe manner so that you do not cause any further harm to yourself. If you find that you are unable to control your worry on your own, seeking the assistance of a mental health expert can help you progressively overcome your fears by addressing the cognitive patterns that are limiting you.

Methods for Discovering Happiness and Serenity Within Yourself:

Is it something that you find yourself thinking about a lot, and is it something that causes you to worry and feel anxious? The state of having an anxious mind is extremely nerve-wracking. Your search for ways to calm your thoughts has brought you to the right place as you have arrived here.

Generally speaking, accepting things in their current state is what brings about a sense of peace for most people; nevertheless, the meaning of this phrase may differ from person to person. When we are in this state, our thoughts and hearts are liberated from the burden of stress that we have been carrying. Once you have achieved a condition of inner peace, you will be able to discover happiness without having to hunt for it outside. Experiences that bring you happiness and a sense of fulfillment are actively sought after by you.

The ability to create inner tranquility is a vital quality that can be developed with constant effort. This ability can be immediately honed by anyone, regardless of their background or circumstances.

- Make some music play.

Music that is calming can make it simpler for children who have attention-deficit/hyperactivity disorder (ADHD) to concentrate and relax. What really counts is that the music is something that you enjoy listening to and that it makes you feel more relaxed. Whenever you are feeling stressed, the most effective and speedy method to relax is to listen to music that you appreciate. It has been established through research that listening to specific genres of music, such as Celtic, Native American, and Indian string instruments, flutes, drums, rain, thunder, and light jazz, can have a comparable effect on the activity of the brain. method that was utilized by pharmaceutical companies If you are anxious to get started, there is no reason to delay it any longer. Use headphones to listen to music that is comparable to this while streaming it.

- Take a moment to relax and focus on taking deep breaths.

One can improve their ability to deal with stress by practicing aware breathing, which involves paying attention to each breath as it enters and exits the body. This helps the mind and body better manage stress.

Focus your attention on your diaphragm and lungs while you take five slow, deep breaths. Maintain this focus throughout the process. When it comes to circumstances that call for peace and quiet, it is a wonderful option because the consequences are almost rapid.

- Delight in a leisurely stroll across a natural environment.

You may relax and feel better by going for a walk outside. This is a great way to do both. While you are on vacation, you should go for a run outside in the sunshine. Concrete should never be used in excess.

A certain number of individuals have a revitalizing impact when they spend time going outside. While you are listening to the soothing sounds of nature, you will find that your problems start to slip away. Taking these recommendations into consideration will eliminate the need for you to travel. You may go for a walk around the block or to a park that is located nearby.

- Relax and take pleasure in the time you spend with your pet.

For the purpose of relieving stress, it is highly recommended to engage in play with a pet. However, the power of touch is generally overlooked, despite the fact that it is an essential component in reducing stress and improving well-being.

After engaging in tactile stimulation with an animal, individuals who have been diagnosed with mental health issues have reported experiencing less depression and anxiety. If you are fortunate enough to have a pet, make sure to keep it near to you. The release of endorphins, which are responsible for a positive mood, will lead to an improvement in your mood. Fifth, make it a priority to get enough rest. In situations where we are worn out and fatigued, nothing goes according to the plan that we have in mind. Every night, make sure you get enough sleep to give your body a chance to recharge. Getting a sufficient amount of sleep each night will enable you to face the following day with more vitality and reduced levels of anxiety. Do you find that you are unable to fall asleep at the times that are recommended for you? Ensure that you continue to follow your nightly routine. In the minutes coming up to bedtime, put away your electronic devices, play some soothing music, and take some time to unwind with a cup of tea for yourself. Your body will be better able to acclimate to the impending sleep if you establish a normal routine for each night. It is possible that putting your mental and physical health first will have a significant influence on the path that your life takes. Take a look at the article titled "How to Get Deep Sleep in 5 Steps Naturally" if you are having problems getting a good night's sleep.

- Make sure to clean the area on a regular basis.

On the other hand, the negative consequences of clutter are the antithesis of the calming impact that a home that is devoid of clutter may have. It appears to be a significant amount of work, doesn't it? Do not do anything in a hurry. Your possessions should be arranged in that order in both your closet and your workstation. Ensure that the clutter in the kitchen and living room is cleaned up. It is up to you to decide whether you will give them away or sell them.

- Having faith

The need for acceptance is of the utmost importance when it comes to matters of mental health. Your mental health could be significantly improved if you acknowledge that life is full of unpredictability and work on developing strategies to deal with it. Learn to differentiate between things that are under your control and those that are not under your control.

- Be present

When you engage in the practice of mindfulness, you direct your whole attention to the here and now by utilizing all five of your senses: smell, taste, sight, and hearing. Let your senses direct your actions. You won't have to worry about or waste as much time thinking about that. To what extent, however, does one go about the process of growing mindfulness? Focusing on a single job at a time and practicing meditative breathing are both essential practices. "The Power of Mindfulness" is available for you to read whenever it is convenient for you.

- Taking Pleasure in Oneself

When people have a high opinion of themselves, they are less likely to be self-aware then they would otherwise be. As a result of the establishment of a sense of tranquility and confidence in our capacities to face the obstacles that life presents, we are more able to accept ourselves in our current state. The decrease in our sentiments of insecurity is accompanied by an increase in the impression of calmness. Loving oneself is not as difficult as one might believe it to be. It is recommended that you give yourself permission to take a lengthy shower, watch a movie, or even just light some candles in your bedroom if you feel the need to relax and decompress. The act of loving oneself does not have to be difficult, but it does need significant effort.

- Always be honest with yourself and tell the truth.

It is a significant problem with regard to the psychological health and contentment of members of the population. When our thoughts and emotions are in agreement with the activities that we take, we are working in a congruent manner. In order to achieve congruence, it is necessary for your internal and outward perceptions of oneself to be in agreement with one another.

It is when our internal views about ourselves, such as being a caring mother, are in contradiction with our outer actions, such as ignoring our children because we are too busy, that we experience discord. Learning how to constantly act in accordance with one's principles is the most important factor in maintaining one's mental health.

Discovering the secrets of the keys to happiness and honesty can help you get the life you deserve.

- Have fun and find joy in your life.

Laugh frequently and let rid of anxiety. As soon as you have mastered the skill of self-deprecating comedy and world-deprecating humor, you will be able to take advantage of instant an improvement. Endorphins and other compounds that are similar to endorphins are released when people laugh, which is one of the reasons why laughter has a calming impact. What exactly is going to be involved in this piece of advice? Do you feel that it is more important to make jokes all the time or to watch ten comedies every single day? Yes, without a doubt not. Changing your perspective requires you to essentially do that first.

- Love that is unconditional and in abundance.

When you don't anticipate receiving something in return, it is much simpler to love without fear. It is possible for a conditional love relationship to culminate in frustration and anger if the expectations of the relationship are not met. Having anxiety makes it difficult for the mind to rest.

Love that is conditional differs significantly from love that is unconditional in a significant way. It is because you have some expectations of the other person that your love for them is conditional instead than unconditional. Within the context of a romantic partnership, conditional love can result in feelings of resentment, disillusionment, conflict, and unhappiness when expectations are not fulfilled.

- Make schedules for routine medical checkups.

You will not achieve your goal of "I want peace of mind" if you continue to repeat the phrase to yourself without taking any steps to achieve it.

Investing in self-care and keeping a close eye on your health is something that is well worth doing. Some people have poor self-esteem, which can be shown by the fact that they do not believe in themselves. One's perspective and the manner in which other people interact with you are both influenced by this. Affirm your gratitude for what you already own and make it a priority to look for yourself.

Just can't seem to find the time to schedule a visit to the doctor? You should make use of modern tools. With a number of apps that are related to health, you can have a virtual session with a doctor.

- Recall the past

At regular intervals, you ought to take a moment to pause and reflect on the degree to which you are content with your life. How much do you take pleasure in your work? What about your romantic relationships? Am I heading in the right direction? Adjustments should be made as necessary in order to obtain inner peace.

Taking stock of your life on a regular basis will assist you in determining what aspects of it require improvement, regardless of how large or small the area may be. Your career, your life, your nutrition, or something else totally could be the subject of this conversation.

- Take the initiative

The point that came before this one, number 14, is pertinent here. When we establish goals for ourselves and work hard to achieve them, we experience a sense of success.

Having objectives, on the other hand, is not enough information. Setting goals that are SMART—that is, specific, measurable, achievable, relevant, and time-bound—will help you achieve the best possible results. Now that these limitations have been implemented, you will be held to a higher standard of responsibility. At times, it is appropriate to make light of the circumstance.

Improve your ability to adapt to changing circumstances. The more unequivocal our beliefs are, the greater the likelihood that we will be confronted with evidence that runs counter to them. It is important to keep in mind that you do not have to be so critical of yourself whenever you become aware that you are.

- Unwind and let life to take its course.

Rather of ruminating on the past or the future, you should draw your attention back to the here and now. Right now is the only opportunity we have.

Our ability to let go of worries about the past or the future is facilitated by our ability to remain in the here and now. In addition, if you concentrate on the here and now, you will be able to experience greater levels of achievement.

The question is, how are you able to inhabit the present moment? Always make it a point to engage in activities that bring you joy on a daily basis. Seize the opportunity to take in the views and sounds of nature, savor the flavor of your meal, and appreciate the nice words of your company. Last but not least, schedule some time in your schedule every day to engage in an activity that brings you pleasure.

Here are some things to think about if you want to free yourself from the burden of thinking about the future and begin living in the here and now.

- Don't upset yourself

Every single day, each and every one of us comes up with approximately 6,000 new ideas, according to estimates. Acknowledging that your worries are unhelpful and will prevent you from ever being at peace is the first step in learning how to "put aside" your worries.

- It is important to have confidence in your skills and recommendations.

There is no doubt that this is one of the most effective methods for calming your racing mind. It is perfectly acceptable for you to come here and express your thoughts, just like it is for everyone else. When we allow ourselves to be influenced by apathetic behavior or passivity, we cause harm to ourselves.

Either being quiet and allowing the desires and requirements of other people to take precedence over your own, or being aggressive and allowing yourself to be neglected, are not characteristics that are associated with assertiveness. Finding a solution that benefits both parties—a "win-win" deal—should be the first objective instead. Being courageous and standing up for what you believe to be right is not a bad thing. You should become skilled at being yourself and discovering ways to express yourself in a strategic manner.

- Let your thoughts be known

Freedom of expression is of the utmost importance. This trait is inextricably linked to the concept of assertiveness. Speak up for what it is that you require and desire. You are not going to get what you want if you don't make your request known to anyone.

Having said that, it is far simpler to say than it is to accomplish. However, it is important to remember that not everyone is comfortable being entirely honest, especially in public settings. Therefore, begin with a little step; for example, suggest that you and your partner go out to eat or watch a movie as a way to spend time together.

- Taking "me time" into consideration is important.

By granting yourself permission to engage in activities that bring you joy, you will strengthen your ability to withstand the ongoing stresses that life brings. It is essential to locate and maintain a healthy equilibrium.

Spending some time in introspection is something you should do if you want to learn more about who you are. You must prioritize your own well-being if you place a high value on your own personal development. What options are available to you at this moment in time? You may go on a vacation by yourself or eat at the restaurant that you enjoy the most. Having time to yourself shouldn't make you feel uncomfortable or weird.

- To put it all together

According to the definition provided by the free online dictionary, "frolic" means "to act in a carefree and playful manner; to frolic." When people are required to labor nonstop, they immediately experience feelings of stress. Find a method to incorporate activities that you enjoy doing. Create a sense of humor out of situations that aren't exactly hilarious. It is important to maintain a light and carefree attitude toward life. How long has it been since you allowed yourself to indulge your inner child and started playing? You may try doing something like dancing in the rain, watching an animated movie, or just taking a few deep breaths if you are having difficulties going to sleep.

- It's time to let go

For some things, it is simply not feasible to change them, regardless of how much work you put into them. When you realize that it is time to quit trying, let go (just like Elsa in the movie!). In order to begin the process of releasing, the first step is to acknowledge the things that you have no control over. Acceptance should be the focus of your attention rather than resistance here. On the moment when you start letting go of the past, you will go through these ten experiences.

- You have no reason to feel embarrassed

One of the most unpleasant and disturbing emotions is guilt. Despite the fact that anger can motivate us (in a negative sense), the negative consequences of anger are extremely significant. According to one study, it may also lead you to experience a sensation of being physically heavier.

You can prevent yourself from putting yourself through needless stress by examining the rationalizations that you use to justify your feelings of guilt. You shouldn't feel awful when your plans finally come to fruition. Remember at all times that there are some things that you simply cannot change or alter in any way.

- Never forget to express gratitude.

When we take a moment to reflect on all the good things that have occurred in our lives, we are able to find a sense of peace and look on the bright side of life. There are times when we need to be gently prodded in order to revitalize ourselves. Taking the time to acknowledge even the most insignificant of occurrences is one method for cultivating an attitude of gratitude. What did you think of your breakfast this morning? I give all the glory to God. What did you think of the commute you took in the morning? Don't forget to show your gratitude. Make a note of the positive things that happened today, regardless of how insignificant they may have been.

- It is important to take a step back from failure and use it as a stepping stone to success

Even though the word "failure" is frequently associated with negative connotations, the reality is that we all experience failure at some point in our lives. If a person never makes a mistake, they will never discover anything new or make any progress. Failure is something that everyone experiences; even the most successful individuals have to deal with it.

An unquestionable method for developing bravery is to keep a positive attitude in the face of challenges and discouragements. It is not your fault at all. The true problem is the actions that you take yourself. There is a huge gap that needs to be filled. After some time has passed, you will develop your skills. It is imperative that you put an end to your fear and give it another shot.

- Engage in meaningful conversation with other people

The ability to have friends and family members who "get" you and can connect to what you are going through is one of the most wonderful aspects of going through life. Whenever we come across someone who is able to empathize with us and establish a connection with them, we experience an overwhelming sense of happiness and comfort. Interact with them, even if it's only to say hi when you first meet them. From this vantage point, you will discover the unexpected potential to foster the establishment of connections.

- To put yourself to the test

Unless you force yourself out of your comfort zone, you will never be able to truly understand your talents. There is an old proverb that says it is better to feel sorry for what you have done than to wish that you had done something else.

Through hopping, you can reach the current level. Continue to test yourself to the edge of your capabilities. Easy strategies to start moving in the right direction include making that long-awaited phone call or introducing yourself to a new acquaintance. Both of these are examples of effective ways to get things started. By putting oneself through challenging situations, the goal is to achieve personal growth. By stepping into unfamiliar area, you can push yourself to the limits of your capabilities. Consider each of these ten strategies in order to achieve this goal.

Experiment using a variety of different ways to communicate your negative feelings

Whatever it is that piques your interest, whether it be sports, hobbies, or online communities of people who share your characteristics. Detrimental feelings should not be ignored because it may have a detrimental impact on your overall health. If you are able to cultivate the ability to redirect your negative feelings in a constructive manner, you will discover happiness and relief.

It is possible to avoid your negative emotions from becoming overwhelming if you are aware of how to handle them before they become overwhelming. Constantly suppressing your feelings will, in the long run, cause you to become exhausted. Whenever you find yourself having negative feelings, it is important to recall the methods you use to let them go.

- Maintain a speed that is reasonable

My understanding of the situation's level of urgency is lacking. All too frequently, we place unnecessary burdens on ourselves by having extremely high expectations. Set aside your annoyance and focus your attention on the events that are taking place at this very moment. The journey to achieving inner serenity starts here. However, why is it so challenging to calm down during this time? Please take your time and exercise caution.

- You should consider making your homework and assignments more difficult.

Through the use of self-imposed tension, it is never possible to achieve inner peace and fulfillment and satisfaction. When you become more proficient at using the word "could" rather than "should," you will have a greater degree of control over your life and will be able to fulfill your own criteria.

The individual's obligations and tasks are the source of any excessive strain or limitation that may be experienced. It is important to remind your inner child that life is not a competition and that you do not have to be the best at everything. In order to feel failure, it is not necessary to compare yourself to other people who have failed.

- Demonstrate a Careful At

Not a single item is lost, yet a great deal of change is possible. By performing acts of kindness, both the giver and the recipient are able to benefit. It is easy to forget that being kind does not cost anything and almost never has negative consequences. This is because we tend to treat ourselves with the same level of kindness that we would provide to a close friend.

If you put even one of these 29 suggestions into practice, performing one act of kindness each and every day will become as natural as breathing to you.

- Comparison

In the process of comparing ourselves to other people, we sacrifice our own authenticity. Set aside the thoughts and behaviors of others who are in your immediate vicinity. What is it that you are looking for? We each travel through life at our own pace, gaining knowledge and understanding in our own unique ways. Life is a trip, and we all take it together.

Your focus should remain on the road in front of you, and you should refrain from second-guessing or worrying about the conduct of other individual drivers. When you spend time comparing things, you deprive yourself of joy. We find satisfaction when we accept our individuality and do not to conform to the expectations of others.

- Proverbs and affirmations focused on the positive

Utilize affirmations to engage in a constructive conversation with yourself. Examples include, "I can handle whatever life throws at me." Oh, that is a fantastic tagline.

Maintain your confidence in yourself and reassure yourself on a regular basis that everything will be fine. You can help yourself recover faith in your ability to regulate your emotions by reminding yourself on a frequent basis of the worth you bring to the world. It was necessary for you to receive additional support in order to believe in yourself. Get unstuck with these ten affirmations that will change your life and help you get unstuck. 35. It is of the utmost importance to ensure that there is a consistent flow of cash into the bank at all times.

You ought to put some money aside for a time when you will truly require it. You should make it a habit to save money whenever it is possible to do so. Establishing a monthly recurring debit will ensure that you will never again have to worry about being short on finances. You should make it a habit to monitor both your income and your expenditures on a monthly basis. If you have a clear view of your current financial situation, you will be able to manage your resources more effectively.

- Eliminating clutter is essential to having a house that is well-organized

When it comes to happiness, money can buy ease, but it cannot buy the happiness that we so desperately want. The cultivation of an attitude of thankfulness for the straightforward joys that life has to offer is the key to long-term happiness. From the moment you start putting this plan into action, you will experience an improvement in both your mental and financial well-being. Invest your money in the things that are most important to you, and eliminate the unnecessary expenses.

- Adherence

Take a step back and try to view the bigger picture rather than concentrating on instant solutions. To what extent do you anticipate that these feelings will last over a period of time? Is it something that you consider to be significant that you are going through right now?

In most cases, you won't experience any difficulties. Provide them with a sense of perspective in order to assist them in relaxing. By shifting your perspective, you will be able to obtain a more accurate image of the wants and desires that you actually have. Remember that there is more to life than what you can see, and never lose sight of that truth. It is important to maintain your attention on the bigger picture and to express gratitude for what we have, but you should not let this gratitude cloud your judgment. You will be able to acquire genuine money if you simply adhere to these guidelines.

- Keep a close eye on the patterns that are occurring in your mind

Our degree of happiness is significantly impacted by the beliefs that we have. Take some time to reflect on the things that bring out the best in you when you want to feel your best. You should hold a conversation with yourself in the same way that you would with a reliable friend or member of your family. It is meaningless to be self-absorbed, because it deprives one of the joys that life has to offer. When it comes to bringing out the best in other people as well as in yourself, the first step is to be kind and loving to yourself. It cannot be denied that you have the right to happiness. A significant portion of how you feel emotionally is determined by what you think. Whatever happens is entirely up to you.

Raise your voice to require a change in the relationship. You should pursue your interests, whether they involve fighting for the rights of animals or providing assistance to those who are in need. You should fight the urge to conform to the standard.

Do not alter who you are in order to conform to the expectations of other people if you wish to maintain your tranquility. It is important to keep in mind that you should always be respectful, even when you are standing up for what you believe in.

- Not the least of the list

Authenticity, acceptance of the fact that life is unpredictable, and the ability to keep one's thoughts under control are all necessary components in the pursuit of inner peace. The majority of us "abuse" our minds on a daily basis by thinking and saying things that are derogatory to ourselves.

If you learn to have less faith in your beliefs, dismiss negative thoughts, and focus on the positive elements of your life, you will be able to achieve a great deal of inner peace.